Norwich medieval churches
as part of the city landscape

David Luckhurst

Lasse Press

Text and illustrations © David Luckhurst
Design © Curran Publishing Services Ltd

All rights reserved. No reproduction, copy or transmission of this publication may be made without written permission.

No portion of this publication may be reproduced, copied or transmitted save with written permission or in accordance with the provisions of the Copyright, Designs and Patents Act 1988, or under the terms of any licence permitting limited copying issued by the Copyright Licensing Agency, Saffron House, 6–10 Kirby Street, London EC1N 8TS.

Any person who does any unauthorized act in relation to this publication may be liable to criminal prosecution and civil claims for damages.

The author has asserted his right to be identified as the author of this work in accordance with the Copyright, Designs and Patents Act 1988.

First published 2017
by the Lasse Press
2 St Giles Terrace, Norwich NR2 1NS, UK
www.lassepress.com
lassepress@gmail.com

ISBN-13: 978-0-9933069-8-3

Typeset in Sari by
Curran Publishing Services Ltd, Norwich, UK

Manufactured in the UK by Cambrian Printers, Aberystwyth

Contents

Map of Norwich showing the location of the medieval churches — iv

Introduction — 1

The churches:

1. St Augustine, St Augustine's Street — 2
2. St Martin at Oak, Oak Street — 3
3. St Mary Coslany, St Mary's Plain — 4
4. St Michael Coslany, Oak Street — 5
5. St George Colegate, Colegate — 6
6. St Clement, Colegate — 7
7. St Edmund, Fishergate — 8
8. St Saviour, Magdalen Street — 9
9. St James, Cowgate — 10
10. St Martin at Palace, Palace Plain — 11
11. St Helen, Bishopgate — 12
12. St Simon and St Jude, Elm Hill — 13
13. St George Tombland, Tombland — 14
14. St Peter Hungate, Princes Street — 15
15. St Mary the Less, Queen Street — 16
16. St Michael at Plea, Redwell Street — 17
17. St Andrew, St Andrew's Street — 18
18. St John Maddermarket, Maddermarket — 19
19. St Gregory, Pottergate — 20
20. St Laurence, St Benedict's Street — 21
21. St Margaret, St Benedict's Street — 22
22. St Swithin, St Benedict's Street — 23
23. St Benedict, Wellington Lane — 24
24. St Giles, Upper St Giles Street — 25
25. St Peter Mancroft, Haymarket — 26
26. St Stephen, Rampant Horse Street — 27
27. All Saints, All Saints Green — 28
28. St John Timberhill, Timberhill — 29
29. St Peter Parmentergate, King Street — 30
30. St Julian, St Julian's Alley — 31
31. St Etheldreda, King Street — 32
32. St John de Sepulchre, Finklegate — 33

The towers of Norwich — 34

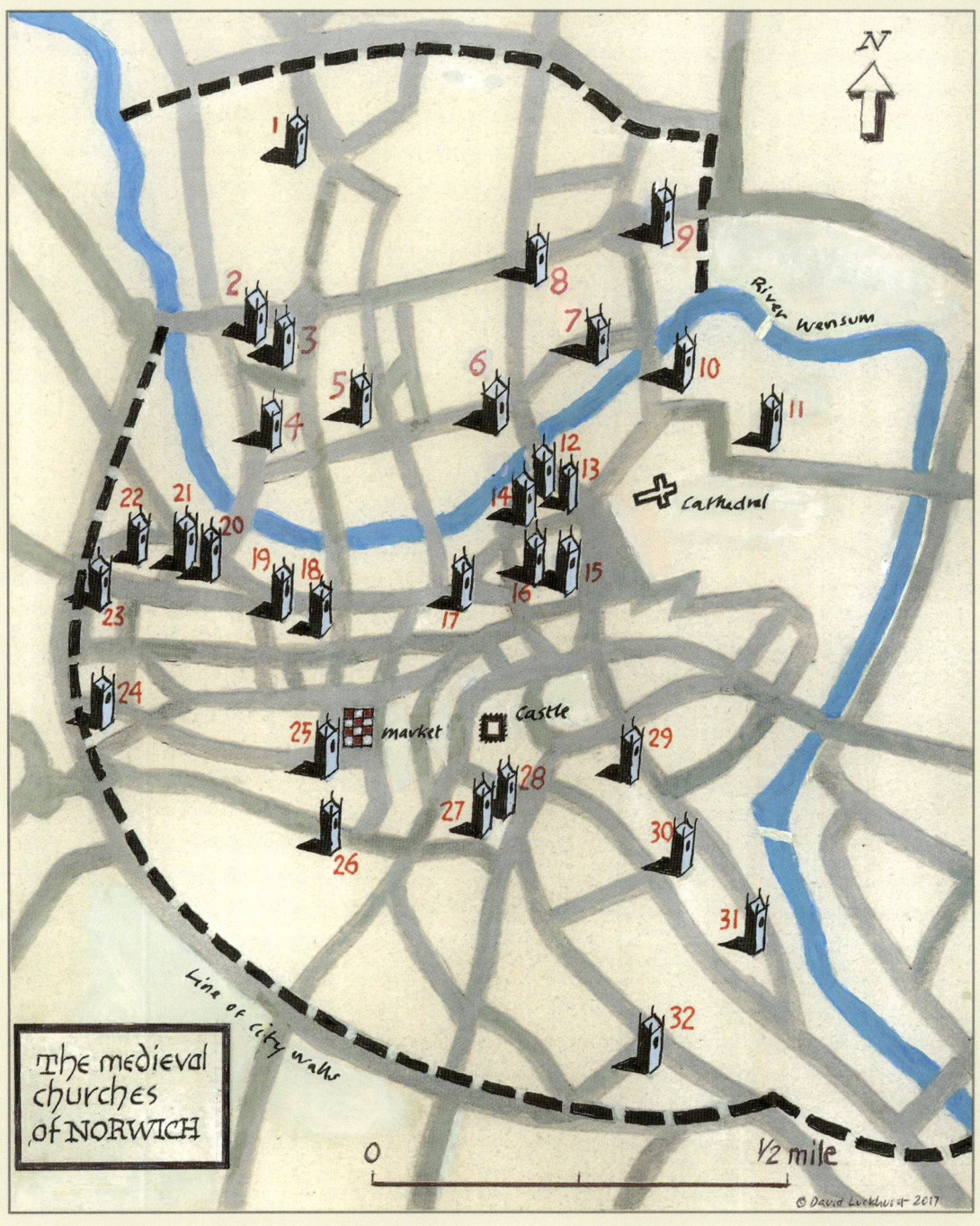

1	St Augustine	2	St Martin at Oak	3	St Mary Coslany	4	St Michael Coslany
5	St George Colegate	6	St Clement	7	St Edmund	8	St Saviour
9	St James	10	St Martin at Palace	11	St Helen	12	SS Simon and Jude
13	St George Tombland	14	St Peter Hungate	15	St Mary the Less	16	St Michael at Plea
17	St Andrew	18	St John Maddermarket	19	St Gregory	20	St Laurence
21	St Margaret	22	St Swithin	23	St Benedict	24	St Giles
25	St Peter Mancroft	26	St Stephen	27	All Saints	28	St John Timberhill
29	St Peter Parmentergate	30	St Julian	31	St Etheldreda	32	St John de Sepulchre

Introduction

This book contains an image of each of the thirty-two medieval churches in Norwich (including the tower of St Benedict) and was inspired by the ongoing UEA/Leverhulme Trust research study of them to improve public awareness of this quite remarkable heritage. It was also an excuse to paint some local urban landscape – as I was to discover, not all of it familiar.

The originals were painted in acrylic on card to A5 size (approx 6×8 in) over roughly a six-month period, in a deliberately colourful picture-postcard style. I have not focused too intensely on the architecture of the individual churches, but sought to portray the diversity of their surroundings within such a compact area. They are presented here with just a short personal observation on each one, to encourage the viewer to absorb the totality in a single visual experience.

Many years ago I pursued a similar objective by drawing all the towers in a single image which my wife and I used as a Christmas card, and this is included at the end.

David Luckhurst
Norwich, 2017

1
St Augustine

St Augustine is the only Norwich medieval church to sport a brick tower, and this only since 1683 when its flint one was refaced. Parallel to the church on its south side is the charming row of 16C Gildencroft cottages running back from busy St Augustines Street, but a path through the churchyard leads to this intimate space and another long residential row, this time on the north side facing the Church Hall. It was designed in the 1970s by Edward Skipper, as successfully in my view as those around St Benedicts Church.

2
St Martin at Oak

A substantial rebuild after wartime bomb damage. Forty years ago I was asked to paint the church in action as Norwich Night Shelter for a flyer. Today this end of St Martin's Lane is almost a village street in an area where far more people live now so many factories have gone. The churchyard is an oasis of green, in summer screening from the artist the curious west front facing Oak Street.

3
St Mary Coslany

In this picture Rosemary Lane leads past the gabled end of 16c Pykerells House, with its 15c hall behind, to St Mary's Plain and its pivotal feature, the cylindrical tower of the church. The tower has Anglo-Saxon belfry openings, and indeed Coslany was one of Norwich's five original Saxon settlements. In its time this area has undergone periodic river flooding, poverty and much German bomb damage.

4
St Michael Coslany

With its ebullient display of flushwork worthy of the 'Antiques Roadshow' St Michael is the acknowledged jewel in the crown of 'Norwich over the Water'. This area was designated by the City's imaginative planner Alfred Wood in the 1970s for residential projects of all kinds to replace industrial development moving out to ring-road sites, now successfully accomplished. Here is a corner of the church's west end beside a colourful row of houses off Oak Street.

5
St George
Colegate

A spectacle, whether viewed from St George Street, Colegate or Muspole Street, thanks to another lofty tower, handsome fenestration and fine big trees in its diminutive churchyard. Yet in 1949 it had to be rescued from near dereliction. Back in 1876 a competing tower was built, part of the bulky shoe factory across the street designed by Edward Boardman for Howlett and White.

6
St Clement

The tall slender tower of St Clement is prominent at the junction of Colegate and Magdalen Street close to Fye Bridge. It makes an impressive climax to the east end of the Friars Quay project, the first to be built in 'Norwich over the Water' in the early 1970s and which I designed with Feilden and Mawson. The forty tall houses occupy a riverside site, facing the Cathedral and in the company of historic buildings of all kinds.

7
St Edmund

A small and unassuming church sporting bold buttresses to its severe tower and a long unbroken roofline. Easily disregarded when in Fishergate these features became readily apparent in this vista along Blackfriars Street, symmetrically framed by buildings of industrial scale and demeanour. The cathedral spire, not so distant, completes this rather theatrical and little-known ensemble.

8
St Saviour

The future necessity for the obtrusive 1960s Magdalen Street flyover has recently been questioned. Its relationship to the traditional street architecture all around has not softened at all with the passage of time, but the chunky tower of St Saviour has never seemed to me to be that bothered.

9
St James

St James's jolly little tower (an 18C brick octagon on top of a cube) is a familiar friend to all users of the inner ring road. Less familiar to them perhaps is this sideways view looking down Whitefriars from the end of Cowgate, revealing quite a noble space in front of the church. This is only spoilt by the asphalt and cars which engendered it but it's waiting for those new trees to grow up a bit.

10
St Martin at Palace

This church's close relationship to the Cathedral, Law Courts and the agreeable houses fronting Palace Plain is impossible to capture in summer because of trees. This more distant view (accompanied by hospitality from the 'Adam and Eve') will hopefully serve as well to depict its setting. The big flint wall to the left encloses Queen Elizabeth Close (sheltered houses) designed by Feilden and Mawson in the 1970s.

11
St Helen

St Helen's Church is part of the Great Hospital complex in Bishopsgate, and is located well to the right of the bold South Tower beneath a roof 200ft long, shared with mens' and womens' dormitories. The exquisite cloister lies invisible behind. Away to the left is the dome and roof of Jarrolds 1839 St James Mill, and facing the playing field are the Norwich School's pavilion and Lower School. Time was when I could watch the cricket from my office desk in Ferry Road until trees by the river became too tall!

12
St Simon and St Jude

With only half of its west tower left a rather sombre presence at the bottom of Norwich's celebrated Elm Hill. It was the subject of repeated ruination and neglect in the 20th century but finally saved by the Norwich Society, and today held together by its concrete first floor. For many years after WW2 it was a Boy Scout centre.

13
St George
Tombland

St George's handsome tower rises up delightfully above the traditional frontages of Princes Street, providing a well-loved accent to the gentle curve of the street. But in this picture on the other side the whole church gets involved, to supply a splendid backdrop to the walk along Tombland Alley rewarding by day or night. Unusually, the clerestory windows are set in brickwork.

14 St Peter Hungate

The current use of this little church as a stained glass museum is admirable, and there's a fine 15C hammerbeam roof inside as well. Externally I dislike the quirky Edwardian slate roof to the tower, but I enjoy those vast windows beyond it and their muscular separating buttresses. The raised churchyard to the north has quite a paddock-like air — one could imagine livestock grazing on it.

15
St Mary
the Less

Set back from public streets this is probably the city's least known medieval church although located right in the centre just yards from the Cathedral. It possesses a tower and a churchyard. Access is occasionally possible on heritage days only as it is used for storage. Here the door to the churchyard off Tombland is unlocked and the tower specially illuminated.

Formerly this view was quite different. St Andrews Street curved left in the distance into Princes Street in front of a four-storey pub (the City Arms) which blocked the view of the church at the top of the hill. The pub came down in 1899 to create a new street enabling trams to climb up to Bank Plain. I have omitted road signs and street lamps to intensify the space, which was widened at this end in the 1960s to accommodate three lanes of traffic.

16
St Michael at Plea

17
St Andrew

Second largest in the city and the only one whose tower is older than its church, which has a fine, airy interior. It is hemmed in on three sides by an interesting street and alleys, one of which contains the Bridewell Museum's fine wall of knapped flint. This contrasts the church's south wall which, perversely for Norwich, is of mainly smooth stone.

18
St John
Maddermarket

The elaborate tower of St John enables it to hold its own with neighbours possessing larger but plainer ones. But the church's most beguiling feature, welding it neatly into the townscape all around, is the public passage beneath the tower. As my picture tries to show it constitutes a dramatic climax to views up Maddermarket Alley and a gateway to something else beyond.

19
St Gregory

The forecourt to the church (once its churchyard) adjacent to a busy pedestrian crossroads is a lively place today, until 1840 dominated by the only spire as far as I know to grace a Norwich church. The streamlined 1930s pub makes another enjoyable contribution to the scene.

20
St Laurence

A big, forlorn, empty church sitting along a steep slope above the Wensum, looking its grandest on this North side. In contrast it's rather an anticlimax from St Benedict appearing to sink into the ground. From the end of Oak Street I can omit the conspicuous tower, spoilt for me by the incongruous Victorian spirelet at one corner.

21
St Margaret

Despite few individual distinguishing features of its own every inch of this handsome moderate-sized church says Norwich. As such it is a valuable element visually in the line-up of medieval churches along St Benedicts. In summer though the numerous trees in the sizeable churchyard obstruct possible vantage points, particularly along the street frontage. Here is a less familiar sneak view of the other side looking up St Margaret's Alley.

22
St Swithin

Once in a deprived area of the city, losing its tower in the 1880s and set back from the main street behind trees, only its transformation from furniture store to Arts Centre has put this very modest church back on the map. But it still manages to add unexpected charm to the new down Ten Bells Lane.

23
St Benedict

This church is sadly not on the UEA study's list of existing churches as it was bombed in 1942 and only the tower remains. However this has not prevented it from becoming the centrepiece of a spacious grassy court enclosed by two-storey flats, an exemplary scheme designed by Edward Skipper in the 1970s for Broadland Housing Association. The straightforward horizontality of the design contrasts admirably with the verticality of the tower, and incidentally is executed in the short-lived oversize metric brick.

24
St Giles

On top of a hill, the church dominates the whole of the west side of the city with a tower 120 ft high, the tallest of the lot and crowned by a distinctive 18c cupola. In winter only, you can glimpse this past brutalist work initiated in the late 1960s by City Architect David Percival. These Vauxhall Street residences combine bold silhouette, colour and texture with a bravura difficult to emulate today.

25
St Peter
Mancroft

Largest of the Norwich churches it is a prominent landmark from many directions (including the pungent juxtaposition of old and new seen from inside the Forum). I chose this view of the church rearing up behind the street market, moved here from Tombland after the Norman Conquest and revamped a few years ago by architect Michael Innes. Things are quiet in my picture because it's Easter Monday.

26
St Stephen

One of my favourites, combining a majestic late-Medieval exterior with its rather unrelated but zany remodelled tower acting as a porch. The superb unbroken range of sixteen big clerestory windows on the south side is conspicuous to observant shoppers leaving the Intu Chapelfield Mall, but in the end I chose a less familiar viewpoint in the spacious churchyard where the surrounding city almost seems to disappear.

27
All Saints

The scene here was once a triangular green surrounded by well-to-do houses, facing a pub and All Saints church on its elevated churchyard. Now beside the church on a January afternoon is the praiseworthy transformation (in my view) of an ugly 1960s office block into a tall new city landmark. Will the new pedestrianisation of All Saints Green (still a work in progress) be as successful?

28
St John
Timberhill

A smallish well-kept church at the top of its hill. The open space in front of the churchyard illustrated here successfully separates the church from its boisterous neighbour Castle Mall to the west. Its west tower fell down in 1784 and was replaced as elsewhere with a Victorian belfry on the roof.

29
St Peter Parmentergate

Like St Peter Mancroft, this St Peter too has a multi-storey vestry projecting from its east end, making a contribution to the varied architecture of King Street. Beyond it is the start of the rewarding climb through the wooded churchyard to Cattle Market Street past the tall, aisle-less church. This is seen here rising above a weekend road race along King Street below.

30
St Julian

The postwar rebuild of St Julian after bombing is nicely understated by John Chaplin — I particularly relish the offbeat location of the new belfry, this time low down on the tower stump rather than up on the roof. The entrance forecourt to this important little church to my mind needs further definition. A new domestic-scale building opposite would create a new courtyard space, shutting off the big adjoining car park and its access.

31 St Etheldreda

The exterior of this church, currently artists' studios, was robustly restored in the 1880s by that prolific Norwich Victorian architect Edward Boardman, including the replacement of its thatched roof with tiles. Unlike many other city churches on sloping sites which follow the contours, this one sits at right-angles to its hill, and is perhaps best glimpsed amidst its trees across a little green beside Rouen Road in the shadow of Normandie Tower.

32
St John
de Sepulchre

The lofty tower of St John looms powerfully over the quarter-mile ascent of Ber Street, but today's Ber Street is not really up for this climax — it's too wide, postwar development on its east side not high enough and too messy to make a picture work. So I have chosen a closer view of this imposing church where things are rather better, briefly illuminated in early morning light.

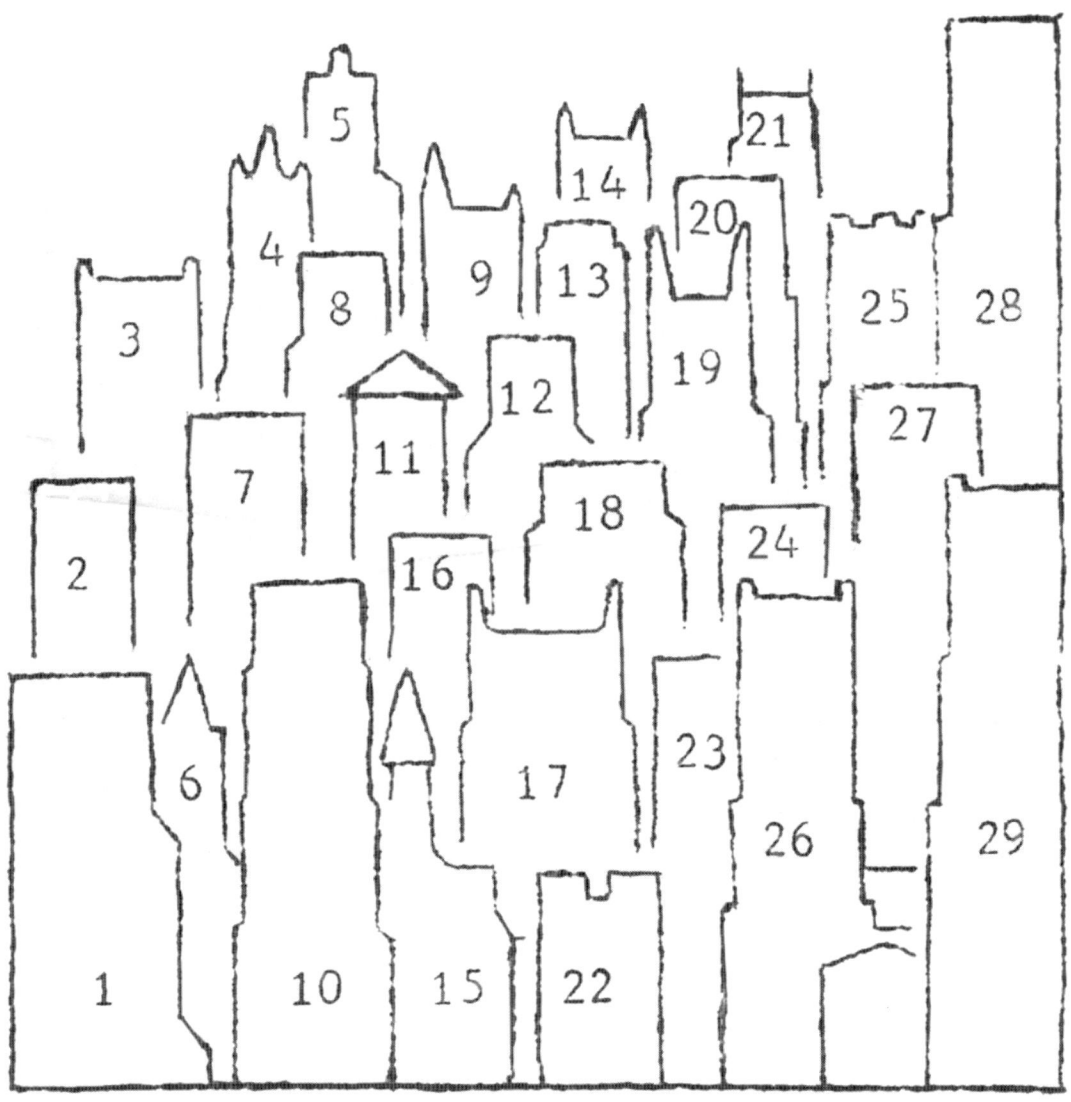

1	St Edmund	2	All Saints	3	St Martin at Palace
4	St Peter Mancroft	5	St Giles	6	St Swithin
7	St Clement	8	St Saviour	9	St Laurence
10	St Stephen	11	St Peter Hungate	12	St Margaret
13	St Augustine	14	St John Maddermarket	15	St John the Baptist
16	St Benedict	17	St Michael Coslany	18	St Mary the Less
19	St Michael at Plea	20	St Helen	21	St John de Sepulchre
22	St James	23	St Mary Coslany	24	St Etheldreda
25	St Peter Parmentergate	26	St George Tombland	27	St Gregory
28	St Andrew	29	St George Colegate		

The Norwich Historic Churches Trust, entrusted with the care of 18 of Norwich's redundant medieval churches, works not only to maintain them but to increase awareness of architectural, historical and other related aspects of our medieval ecclesiastical heritage. These two volumes draw on papers from its 2014 and 2015 conferences, supplemented with a series of contributions about the Trust itself. *Of Churches, Toothache and Sheep* focuses on historical issues; *Redundancy and Renewal* on the problems of the buildings today. Both take a readable and wide-ranging view, stretching well beyond Norwich itself. All profits from the sale of both books go to support the work of the NHCT.

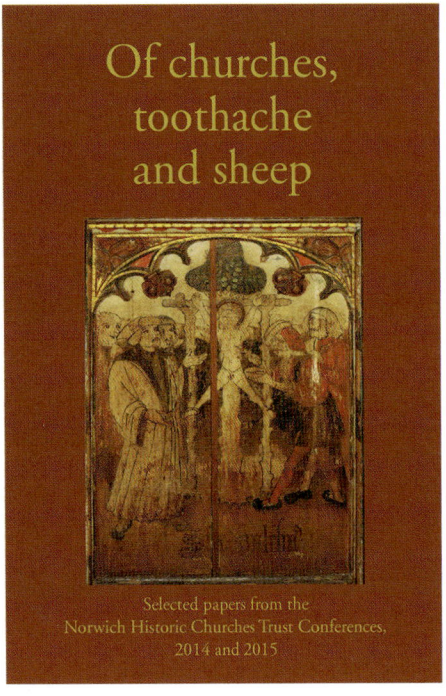

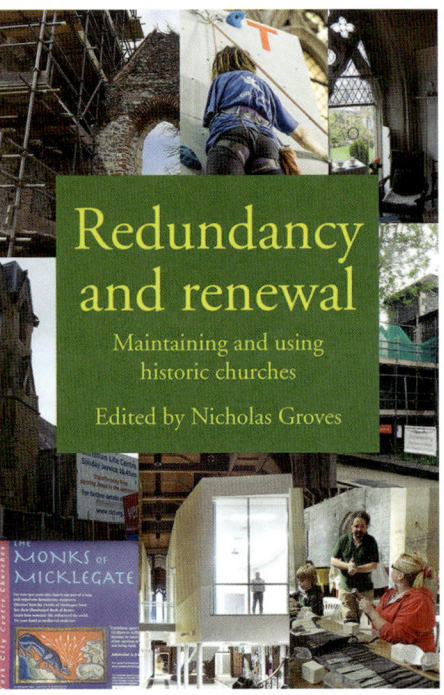

Contents:

Foreword *Brian Ayers;* Preface *Nicholas Groves;* Toothache, saints, and churches in medieval Norfolk, with particular reference to the City of Norwich *John Beal;* Theology to liturgy: the material culture of change in Norwich and beyond, c.1450–1600 *Victor Morgan;* Norwich's Catholic chapels *Francis Young;* The sheep hath paid for all: church building and self-expression in the Late Middle Ages *Allan Barton;* Valuations of churches in medieval Norfolk *Elizabeth Gemmill;* The funeral of John Paston *Susan Curran*

Contents:

Foreword *Nick Williams;* Preface *Nicholas Groves;* Historic churches: heritage and voluntary action *Robert Piggott;* A historical perspective on the reappropriation of urban closed churches for other purposes *Steven Saxby;* Working co-operatively with closed churches: the Holland Coastal Group *Stella Jackson;* 'With concern, but not without hope': an overview of the Norwich Historic Churches Trust *Nicholas Groves;* The Norwich Historic Churches Trust, returning churches to the community *Rory Quinn;* Heavenly Gardens *George Ishmael;* Confessions of a former tenant *Susan Curran;* New uses for religious heritage at the Churches Conservation Trust *Peter Aiers, Matthew McKeague and Edward Walkington*

For full details of these and other Lasse Press titles, visit

www.lassepress.com